W9-AFJ-360

BOSTON
RED SOX

STARS, STATS, HISTORY, AND MORE!

BY K. C. KELLEY

The Child's World®
childsworld.com

Published by The Child's World®
1980 Lookout Drive • Mankato, MN 56003-1705
800-599-READ • www.childsworld.com

Copyright © 2019 by The Child's World®
All rights reserved. No part of this book may be
reproduced or utilized in any form or by any means
without written permission from the publisher.

ISBN 9781503828179
LCCN 2018944830

Printed in the United States of America
PAO2392

Photo Credits:
Cover: Joe Robbins (2).
Interior: AP Images: Amy Sancetta 19, Paul Benoit 23;
Newscom: Jim Ruymen/UPI 5, Chris Lee/MCT 17, Juan
Salas/Icon SW 27; Joe Robbins: 6, 10, 13, 14, 20, 24, 29.

About the Author

K.C. Kelley is a huge sports
fan who has written more
than 100 books for kids. His
favorite sport is baseball.
He has also written about
football, basketball, soccer,
and even auto racing! He lives
in Santa Barbara, California.

On the Cover

Main photo: All-Star Mookie Betts
Inset: Hall of Fame hero
Ted Williams

CONTENTS

GO, RED SOX!

In recent seasons, the Boston Red Sox have been one of baseball's best teams. That was not always true. The Sox have been playing for almost 120 years. Boston went without a title for 86 years . . . in a row. When they finally won again in 2004, Red Sox fans went wild! It was one of the biggest sports stories of the 2000s! The Red Sox also won in 2007, 2013, and 2018! What new stories will the Red Sox tell? Let's meet the Boston Red Sox!

The Red Sox captured the 2018 World Series trophy. ➤
They beat the Los Angeles Dodgers in five games.

WHO ARE THE RED SOX?

he Red Sox play in the American League (AL). That group is part of Major League Baseball (MLB). MLB also includes the National League (NL). There are 30 teams in MLB. The winner of the AL plays the winner of the NL in the **World Series**. The Red Sox went a long time between World Series wins. They won in 1918, but not again until 2004!

◄ *Chris Sale is the star of the Red Sox pitching staff.*

WHERE THEY CAME FROM

In 1901, the AL played its first season. Boston was home to one of the teams. That team was called the Americans. In 1903, Boston's team won the first World Series! In 1908, the team changed its name to the Red Sox. In 1918, they won their fifth World Series! After that, they went a long time without winning another. The Boston club is one of only four original AL teams still playing in the same city.

This is a scorecard from the 1903 World Series, which Boston won. ➤

SOUVENIR CARD 10 CENTS

McGREEVY

On the Avenue

Nuff said . . . .

3rd Base

1903

..SOUVENIR CARD..

OF THE

World's Championship Games

Boston vs. Pittsburg

9

WHO THEY PLAY

The Red Sox play in the AL East Division. The other teams in the AL East are the Baltimore Orioles, the New York Yankees, the Tampa Bay Rays, and the Toronto Blue Jays. The Red Sox play more games against their division rivals than against other teams. In all, Boston plays 162 games each season. They play 81 games at home and 81 on the road. Their biggest **rivals** are the Yankees.

◄ *Shortstop Xander Bogaerts is one of the top young Red Sox stars.*

WHERE THEY PLAY

Fenway Park is the oldest MLB ballpark still in use. It opened in 1912. It has been improved over the years. Still, it looks a lot like it did when the first games were played there. Fenway is famous for its brick walls outside. Inside, its left-field wall is huge. It is called the Green Monster. Players often hit balls that bounce off the wall for hits!

Signs inside Fenway Park celebrate the team's many championships. ➤

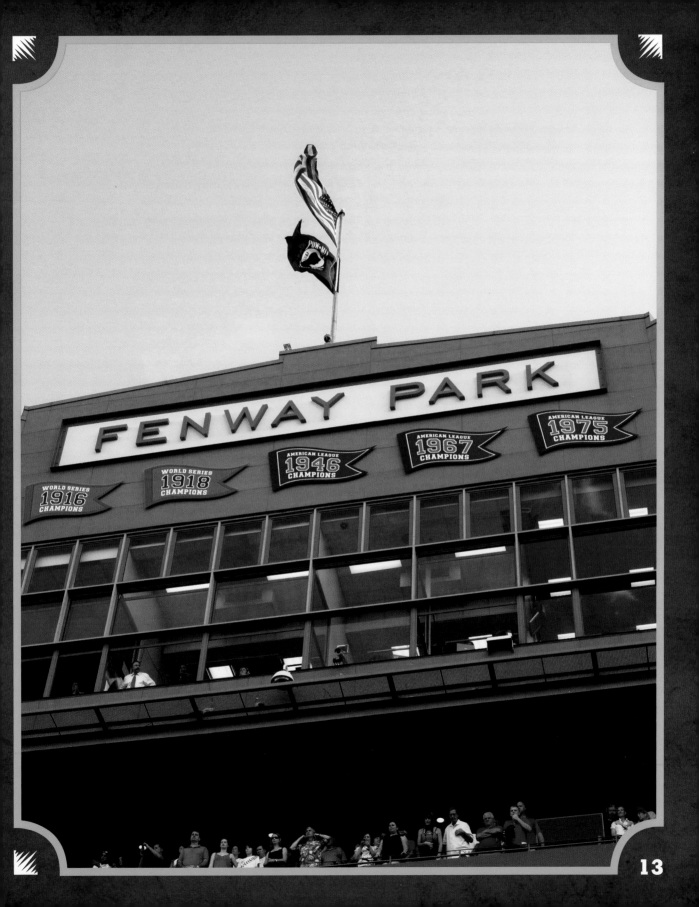

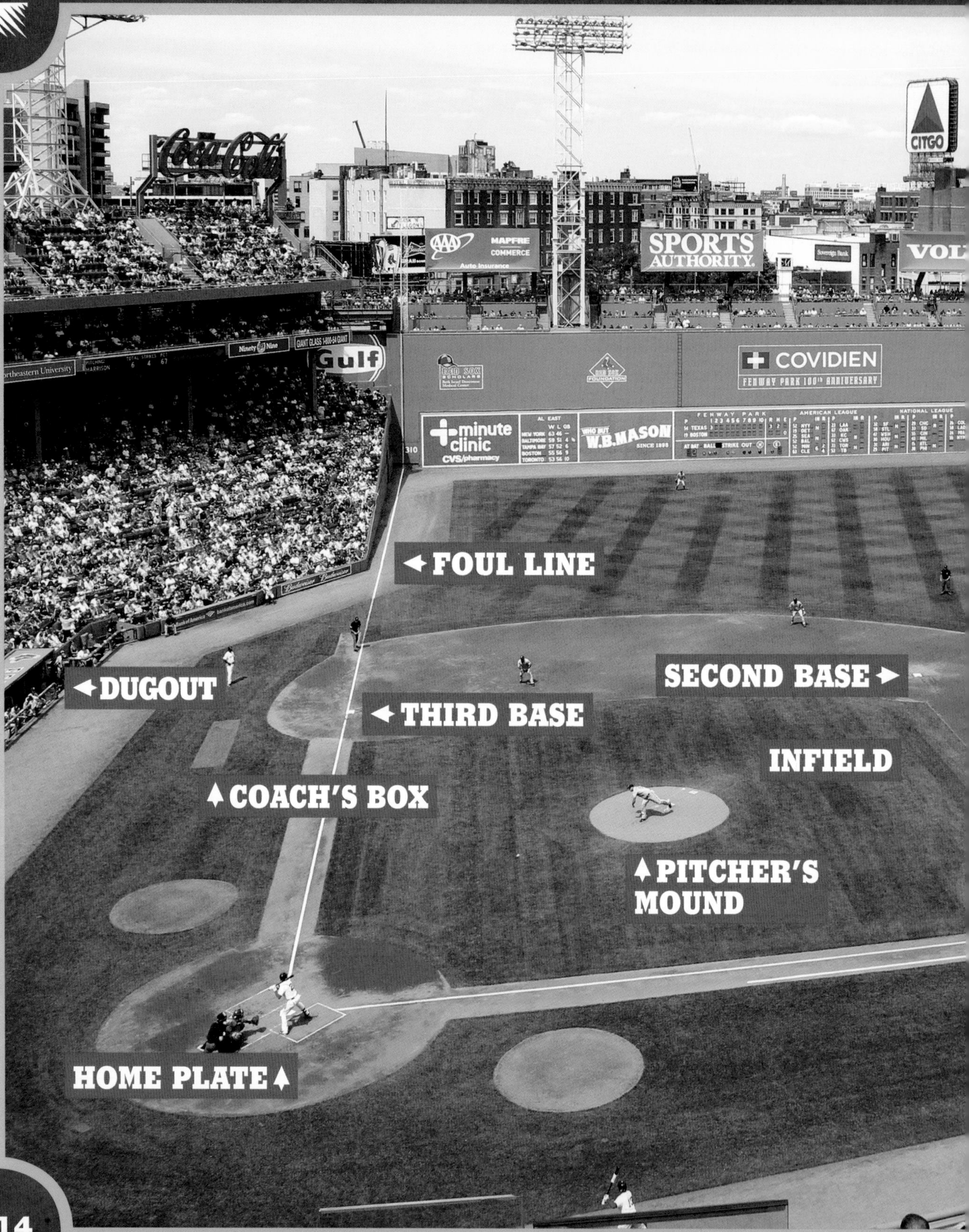

◄ FOUL LINE

SECOND BASE ►

◄ DUGOUT

◄ THIRD BASE

INFIELD

⬆ COACH'S BOX

⬆ PITCHER'S MOUND

HOME PLATE ⬆

THE BASEBALL FIELD

OUTFIELD

FOUL LINE

FIRST BASE

BIG DAYS

The Red Sox have had a lot of great days in their long history. Here are a few of them.

1903—For the first time, the AL and NL champs met in the World Series. Boston beat the Pittsburgh Pirates to win the first title!

2004—Red Sox fans rejoiced! Eighty-six years after their last title, the Red Sox won the World Series. They beat the St. Louis Cardinals in four games.

2018—Boston's great run continued. They won their fourth World Series since 2004. They also set a team record with 108 wins in the season.

Manager John Farrell holds the 2013 World ➤ Series championship trophy.

TOUGH DAYS

Like every team, the Red Sox have had some not-so-great days, too. Here are a few their fans might not want to recall.

1948—The Red Sox and the Indians tied for the best record in the AL. They had a one-game playoff. Cleveland won, disappointing Red Sox fans.

1978—In mid-August, the Red Sox had a huge lead over the Yankees in the AL East. Then New York got hot, and Boston cooled off. The Yankees caught the Red Sox and made the playoffs.

Boston fans were sad as they watched the Mets ➤
celebrate winning the 1986 World Series.

1986—In Game 6 of the World Series, the Red Sox led the Mets. If Boston won the game, it would win the World Series! Then New York scored three runs and won the game! The Mets then won Game 7 to win the Series.

AAA
Auto Insurance

SPORTS
AUTHORITY | UNDER ARMOUR

RED SOX
SCHOLARS
Beth Israel Deaconess
Medical Center

RED SOX
FOUNDATION

FENWA

310

TEX

WHO BUT
W.B. MASON
SINCE 1898

AL EAST			
	W	L	GB
NEW YORK	57	33	—
TAMPA BAY	55	35	2
BOSTON	52	39	5 ½
TORONTO	46	45	11 ½
BALTIMORE	29	61	28

FENWAY PARK
P 1 2 3 4 5 6 7 8 9 10 R
36 TEXAS
31 BOSTON

AT BAT · BALL ▪ STRIKE · OUT · (H)

MEET THE FANS!

Boston fans are known as the "Fenway Faithful." They fill their beloved ballpark game after game. During one stretch, they bought every seat for 820 straight games. That is the longest **sellout** streak ever! In 2011, the Red Sox added seats on top of the Green Monster. Fans have a new birds-eye view of the action! Fenway is also famous for busy nearby streets on game days. Fans come to eat, shop, and visit before watching their team!

◄ *The Green Monster looms over Fenway Park. Seats on top of the wall give fans a great view.*

HEROES THEN

Boston has seen a parade of great players. As a pitcher, Babe Ruth helped the team win three World Series. Later, he was a home run slugger for the Yankees! Ted Williams was called the greatest hitter of all time. He hit .406 in 1941. Carl "Yaz" Yastrzemski led the Red Sox to the 1967 World Series. He won the **Triple Crown** that year! Jim Rice was a star outfielder in the 1970s and 1980s. Pitcher Pedro Martinez was a big part of two Red Sox World Series wins. **Designated hitter** (DH) David Ortiz inspired many with his great hitting and leadership.

Carl Yastrzemski was honored in 1979 when ➤
he got his 3,000th career hit.

HEROES NOW

The Red Sox have one of the best teams in baseball. **Leadoff hitter** Mookie Betts is the key. He gets on base, but he also hits a lot of home runs. DH J.D. Martinez often clubs balls over the Green Monster. Young Andrew Benintendi is a rising star. Pitcher Chris Sale has led the AL in strikeouts three times. Craig Kimbrel is an All-Star **closer**.

◄ *Mookie Betts is one of the best all-around players in baseball.*

GEARING UP

Baseball players wear team uniforms. On defense, they wear leather gloves to catch the ball. As batters, they wear hard helmets. This protects them from pitches. Batters hit the ball with long wood bats. Each player chooses his own size of bat. Catchers have the toughest job. They wear a lot of protection.

THE BASEBALL

The outside of the Major League baseball is made from cow leather. Two leather pieces shaped like 8s are stitched together. There are 108 stitches of red thread. These stitches help players grip the ball. Inside, the ball has a small center of cork and rubber. Hundreds of feet of yarn are tightly wound around this center.

CATCHER'S MASK
AND HELMET ◄

◄ CHEST
PROTECTOR

WRIST ↗
BANDS

CATCHER'S
MITT

SHIN GUARDS ►

CATCHER'S GEAR

TEAM STATS

Here are some of the all-time career records for the Boston Red Sox. All these stats are through the 2018 regular season.

STRIKEOUTS	
Roger Clemens	2,590
Tim Wakefield	2,046

RBI	
Carl Yastrzemski	1,844
Ted Williams	1,839

BATTING AVERAGE	
Ted Williams	.344
Wade Boggs	.338

STOLEN BASES	
Harry Hooper	300
Tris Speaker	267

WINS	
Roger Clemens	192
Cy Young	192

SAVES	
Jonathan Papelbon	219
Bob Stanley	132

Ted Williams was one of the greatest hitters in baseball history.

HOME RUNS	
Ted Williams	521
David Ortiz	483

GLOSSARY

closer (KLO-zer) a pitcher who comes in to get the final few outs of a close game

designated hitter (DEZ-ig-NATE-ed HIT-ter) a player in a baseball lineup who bats instead of the pitcher

leadoff hitter (LEED-off HIT-ter) the player who bats first in a baseball lineup

rivals (RYE-vuhlz) two people or groups competing for the same thing

sellout (SEL-owt) when every ticket to a sporting event is sold

Triple Crown (TRIP-uhl KROWN) not an official award, but a term for a player who leads his league in batting average, home runs, and RBI in the same season

World Series (WURLD SEE-reez) the annual championship of Major League Baseball

FIND OUT MORE

IN THE LIBRARY

Connery-Boyd, Peg. *Boston Red Sox: Big Book of Activities*. Chicago, IL: Sourcebooks, Jabberwocky, 2016.

Tavares, Matt. *There Goes Ted Williams: The Greatest Hitter Who Ever Lived*. Boston, MA: Candlewick, 2015.

Tustison, Matt. *12 Reasons to Love the Boston Red Sox*. Mankato, MN: 12-Story Library, 2016.

ON THE WEB

Visit our website for links about the Boston Red Sox:
childsworld.com/links

Note to Parents, Teachers, and Librarians: We routinely verify our web links to make sure they are safe and active sites. So encourage your readers to check them out!

INDEX